GRAPHIC TRADE SYMBOLS
BY GERMAN DESIGNERS

from the 1907 Klingspor Catalog by

F.H. Ehmcke

DOVER PUBLICATIONS, INC., NEW YORK

Published in Canada by General Publishing Company, Ltd., 30 Lesmill Road, Don Mills, Toronto, Ontario.

Published in the United Kingdom by Constable and Company, Ltd., 10 Orange Street, London WC 2.

Graphic Trade Symbols by German Designers, first published by Dover Publications, Inc., in 1974, is a new selection of pages from *Gildenzeichen Nach Entwürfen von F. H. Ehmcke und Mitarbeitern ausgeführt und herausgegeben durch die Schriftgiesserei Gebr. Klingspor Offenbach-Main* (Trade Symbols from Designs Executed by F. H. Ehmcke and Associates, and Published by the Klingspor Brothers Type Foundry, Offenbach am Main), 1907. For further details, see Publisher's Note.

DOVER *Pictorial Archive* SERIES

Graphic Trade Symbols by German Designers belongs to the Dover Pictorial Archive Series. Up to ten illustrations from this book may be reproduced on any one project or in any single publication free and without special permission. Wherever possible, please include a credit line indicating the title of this book, author and publisher. Please address the publisher for permission to make more extensive use of illustrations in this book than that authorized above.

The reproduction of this book in whole is prohibited.

International Standard Book Number: 0-486-21671-3
Library of Congress Catalog Card Number: 74-75627

Manufactured in the United States of America
Dover Publications, Inc.
180 Varick Street
New York, N.Y. 10014

Publisher's Note

The outset of the twentieth century witnessed a renewal of vitality in every phase of graphic art in Germany. Typography, book design and advertising art received special attention. One of the principal innovators in commercial graphics was Fritz Hellmut Ehmcke, who was strongly influenced by William Morris' ideals of high artisanship in book printing. Ehmcke designed bookplates, posters, ads, book ornament, type faces, furniture and houses, and taught at various art schools.

One of Ehmcke's outstanding achievements was published in 1907, when he was 29. This was a collection of 314 trade symbols, in which he aimed to restore the dignity and monumentality of Renaissance symbols, while making full use of the most vigorous and promising techniques and trends of contemporary art. The result was decades ahead of its time, truly epoch-making and still a revelation today. The symbols initialed "F. H. E." were designed by Ehmcke himself, the others by associates who are not named in the original edition.

The collection was published as a catalog by the Klingspor Brothers Type Foundry (Schriftgiesserei Gebr. Klingspor) in Offenbach. This firm, founded in 1842 as the Rudhard Type Foundry, was acquired by Carl Klingspor in 1892. The plant achieved its great celebrity under his sons Karl (1868-1950) and Wilhelm (died 1925), who assumed the direction in 1895. From 1906, the year before the publication of these trade symbols, the company was known as Klingspor Brothers. In 1956 the business, along with its world-famous types, was acquired by the Frankfurt type founder D. Stempel.

The present edition contains 293 of the symbols from the original publication; two pages containing 21 national, military and patriotic symbols of the era of Kaiser Wilhelm II have been omitted as possessing only antiquarian interest. Furthermore, in the present volume the symbols appear only once each (that is, all repetitions in different sizes are omitted), but all are enlarged to augment their effectiveness and to emphasize their fine detailing. The page layouts of the original book have been retained; in these layouts the symbols are grouped solely by shape and visual congruity, without regard for subject matter or any other principle of arrangement. Identifying captions in English have been provided on each page of symbols, and the alphabetical Index of Trades that follows this Note will permit speedy location of every motif. These captions and Index replace the alphabetical price list (in German) of the original catalog. The trades have been expressed in English as activities (e.g., agriculture), production sites (e.g., spinning mill) or products (e.g., hats); the use of (let us say) "hats," rather than "hatter" or "hat seller," makes it clear that the symbol can be used by any one connected with the given industry. In addition to trades, there are also a few motifs representing certain holidays and festive occasions.

The sample layouts (that is, visual examples of the use of the symbols on announcements, ads, trade cards, envelopes, menus and business forms), which preceded the section of symbols in the original catalog, now follow the symbols.

The following items occurring in the original edition (all in German) have been omitted here: a quotation from Emerson, an introduction offering a very brief historical survey of trade symbols (better information is available elsewhere), and a list of the type faces used in the sample layouts.

Index of Trades

1: Agriculture. 2: Bakery (pretzels are shown). 3: Beekeeping. 4: Ropemaking. 5: Mining.
6: Gardening. 7: Stationery. 8: Lithography ("the stones speak"). 9: Pharmacy.
10: Metalware. 11: Cleaning and pressing. 12: Brickmaking.

13: Carpentry. 14: Architecture. 15: Masonry. 16: Soap and candles (the soap wrapper reads: "Violet"). 17: Bookbinding (shows sewing frame). 18: Printing. 19: Tailoring. 20: Roofing. 21: Horse shoeing. 22: Wagon making. 23: Barrel making. 24: Artistic ironwork.

25: New Year's Eve (legend reads: "Happy New Year!") 26: Stonecutting. 27: Spinning mill. 28: Chinaware. 29: Watchmaking. 30: Toys. 31: Commerce ("debit" and "credit"). 32: Music. 33: Polo. 34: House painting. 35: Millinery, or Featherworking. 36: Weaving.

37: Pharmacy. 38: Nursing. 39: Bell foundry. 40: Pastry, or Coffee house. 41: Coffee house.
42: Fruit. 43: Chess. 44: Bowling. 45: Tennis. 46 & 48: Gymnastics (with oak wreath clusters).
47: Prussian army symbol.

49: Carnival. 50: Mountaineering. 51: Costumes. 52: Photography. 53: Dance.
54: Commerce (Mercury, god of trade). 55: Toys. 56: Fishing. 57: Christmas.

58: Saddlery. 59: Bakery. 60 & 63: Flour (63 has border of grain). 61: Metalworking.
62: Draperies, or Braidmaking. 64 & 66: Upholstered furniture. 65: Shoes.

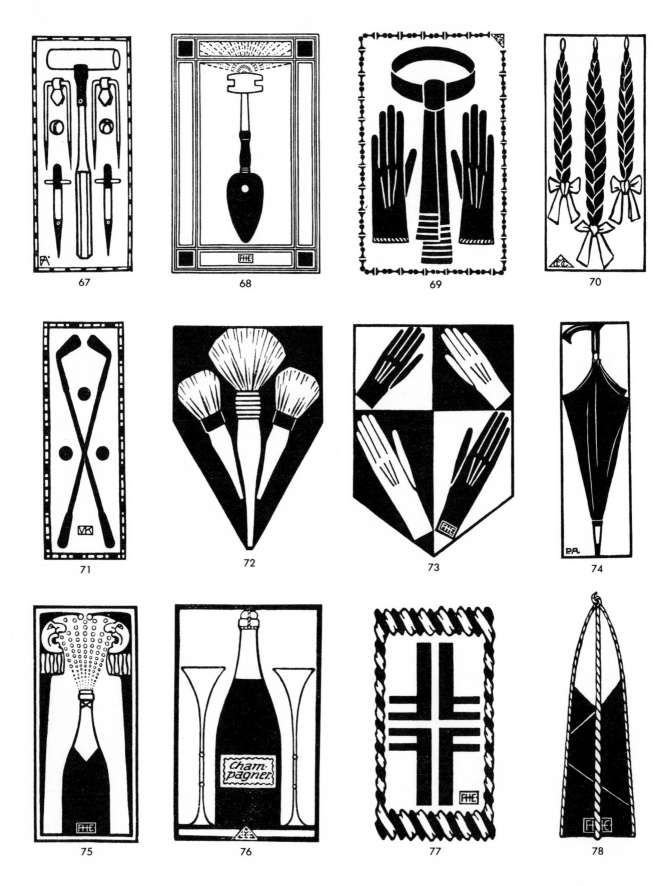

67: Croquet. 68: Glaziery. 69: Ties and gloves. 70: Barber shop, or Hairpieces. 71: Golf.
72: Brushes. 73: Gloves. 74: Umbrellas. 75: Carnival, or Champagne. 76: Champagne.
77: Gymnastics. 78: Spices.

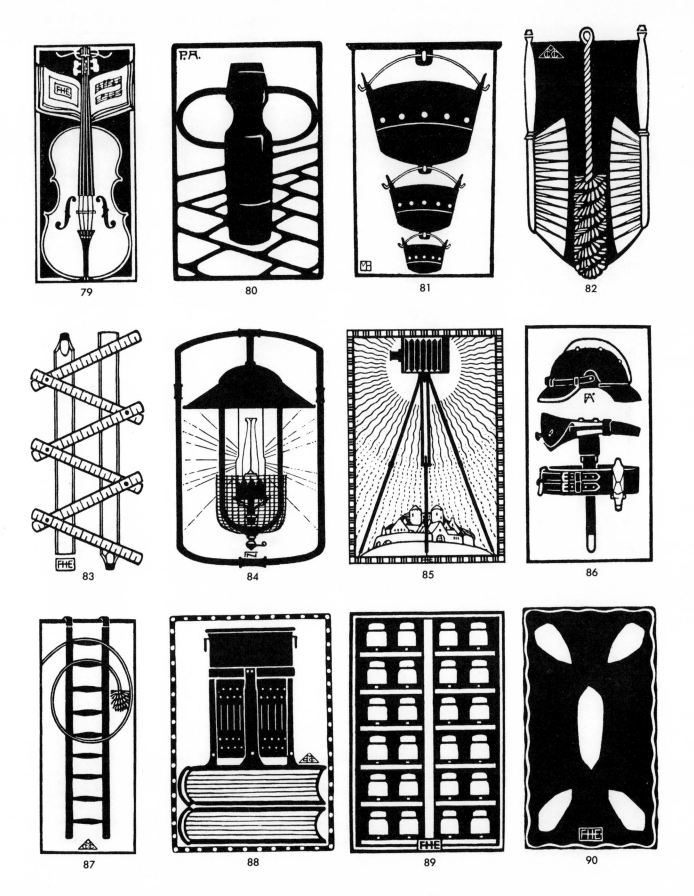

79: Musical instruments. 80: Paving. 81: Copperware. 82: Brushes. 83: Carpentry.
84: Gaslight. 85: Photography. 86: Fire department. 87: Chimney sweeping.
88: Bookbinding (shows gluepot). 89: Telegraph. 90: Gingerbread.

91: Skiing. 92: Horseback riding. 93: Printing (eagle symbol). 94: Opera, Drama, Theater. 95: Literature. 96: Theater. 97: Geography. 98: Watchmaking. 99: Travel.

100: Glassware. 101: Fishing. 102: Gravestones. 103: Stained glass. 104: Zithers. 105: Organs.
106: Cutlery. 107: Wallpaper. 108: Pianos.

109: Party decorations. 110: Mail, or Post (carrier pigeons). 111: Viticulture. 112: Rowing.
113: Printing. 114: Stenography. 115: Shipping lines. 116: Gasworks.

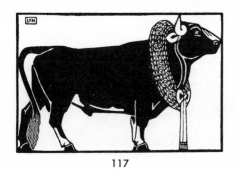

117

118

119

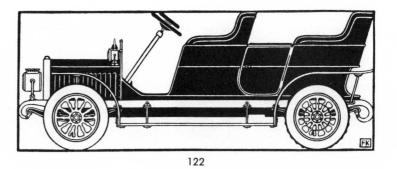

120

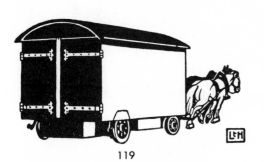

121

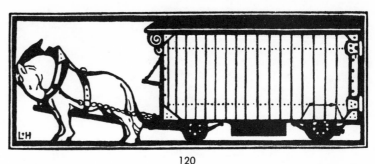

122

123

117: Cattle raising. 118: Funerals. 119 & 120: Moving vans. 121: Horses. 122: Automobiles.
123: Railroads.

124: Flowers. 125: Chinaware. 126: Playing cards. 127: Cigars and pipes. 128: Chemistry. 129: Astronomy. 130: Shorthand. 131: Mail, or Post (posthorn).

132: Bicycles. 133: Luggage. 134: Combs and brushes. 135: Barber shop. 136: Funerals.
137: Poison. 138: Bridge building. 139: Dockyard.

140 & 146: Sailing. 141: Steamboat. 142: Machinery. 143: Navy, or Merchant marine.
144, 147, 148: Shipping lines. 145: Airships. 149: Compasses. 150: Swimming.
151: Ocean commerce.

152: Optical instruments. 153: Locksmithing. 154: Applied art. 155 & 157: Railroads.
156: Carpentry. 158: Mechanical trades. 159: Athletics. 160: Weapons. 161: Electricity.
162: Engineering. 163: Electrical engineering.

164: Red Cross. 165: Barber shop. 166: Bandagist. 167: Stockings. 168: Combs and brushes.
169: Cricket. 170: Engraving. 171: Hats. 172: Oriental wares. 173: Gingerbread. 174: Lottery.
175: Games of chance.

176 & 183: Theater. 177, 185, 187: Music. 178: Commerce (Mercury). 179: Art. 180: Painting.
181: Stonecutting. 182 & 184: Sculpture. 186: Poetry.

188: Butter and cheese. 189: Butcher shop, or Abattoir. 190: Pork butcher.
191: Basketmaking. 192: Billiards. 193: Butcher shop, or Delicatessen.
194 & 195: Bock beer. 196: Beer. 197-199: Tavern.

200, 202, 203, 205: Poultry. 201: Feather beds. 204: Agriculture. 206 & 208: Lightning rods.
207: Funerary monuments. 209: Edelweiss. 210 & 211: Flowers.

212: Coffee. 213: Gingerbread. 214: Tea. 215: Cigarettes. 216: Shoemaking (Crispin is patron
saint of the trade). 217: Cigars. 218: Snuff. 219: Dance. 220: Tobacco, or Pipes.
221: Masked ball. 222: Carnival. 223: Carousel.

224 & 226: Chimney sweeping (the card in 224 reads: "Happy New Year!").
225: Automobiles. 227: Wrestling. 228: Circus. 229: Ice skating. 230: Mail, or Post.
231 & 232: Christmas ("Glory to God in the Highest" and the Three Wise Men). 233: Fishing.
234 & 235: Auctions.

236: Furs. 237: Circus. 238: Millinery. 239: Leather goods. 240: Bakery. 241: Meat supplier, or Butcher shop. 242: Easter. 243: Fishing (as sport).

244: Phonographs (the music is "Deutschland, Deutschland über alles").
245: Carriage building. 246: Swimming. 247: Bicycles.
248: Lottery (the pig refers to the German expression *Glücksschwein*, meaning "lucky mascot").
249: Music. 250: Dentistry. 251: Shoes.

252 & 253: Funerary monuments. 254: Pharmacy. 255: Eggs. 256: Braidmaking.
257: Dairy products. 258: Dog training. 259: Ovens. 260: Circus.

261: Lottery. 262: Basketmaking. 263: Mining. 264: Easter. 265 & 266: Christmas.
267: Perfume. 268: Woolen goods. 269: Shoes.

270: Pastry. 271: Butcher shop. 272: Wood turning. 273: Music. 274: Waiter.
275: Cook. 276: Dyeing. 277: Bicycles. 278: Frames. 279: Birds, or Pet shop.
280: New Year's Eve (punch bowl; "Happy New Year!"). 281: Fruit.

282: Criticism. 283: Jewelry. 284: Fencing. 285: Game and poultry. 286: Mountaineering.
287: Soccer. 288: Tanning. 289: Machinery and tools. 290: Torches, or Illumination. 291: Furs.
292: Horses. 293: Hunting (the stag seen by St. Hubert).

BUCHDRUCKEREI HEINRICH RIEGER

BINGEN AM RHEIN BISMARCKPLATZ 8

EUGEN HEINE
CHARLOTTENBURG
MARSSTRASSE 25

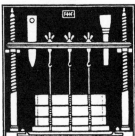

ÜBERNIMMT DIE HER-
STELLUNG FEINSTER
BUCHEINBÄNDE MIT
UND OHNE PRÄGUNG

Oskar Baude
Bürstenlager

Barmen
Tannen=
Straße 4

G. Widel
Fabrik feinster
Pinselwaren
Nürnberg
Markt 7

EINLADUNG
*zum Liebesmahl des
Offizierkorps des 63.
und 27. Feldartillerie-
Regiments in Mainz*

SEDANFEIER DES
KRIEGERBUNDES
ZU KÖNIGSBERG

EINTRITTSKARTE 1.50 MARK

SCHLESISCHER
HÜTTENVEREIN
MITGLIEDER-KARTE

Bock!
Der Ausschank
begann heute!
Karl Markard

 Met deze hebben wy de eer U te berichten, dat onze sedert 1861 gevestigde zaak 1. Juli a. s. ver= plaatst wordt naar Hoogwal 12. Wy zeggen U beleefd dank vor het tot heden ons geschon= ken vertrouven en rleien ons, Uwe geëerde orders ook aan het nieuwe adres te mogen ontvangen. Ons Telefoon=Nummer is 9894. Met de meeste Hogachting NED. dw. dienerren **K. van der Hoog & Zonen, Tailleurs.**

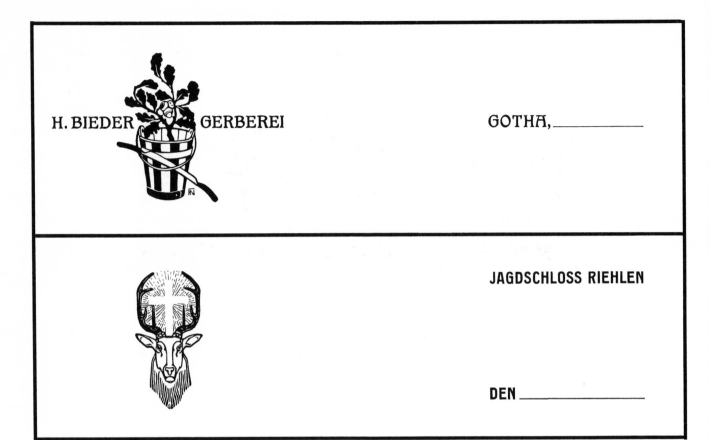

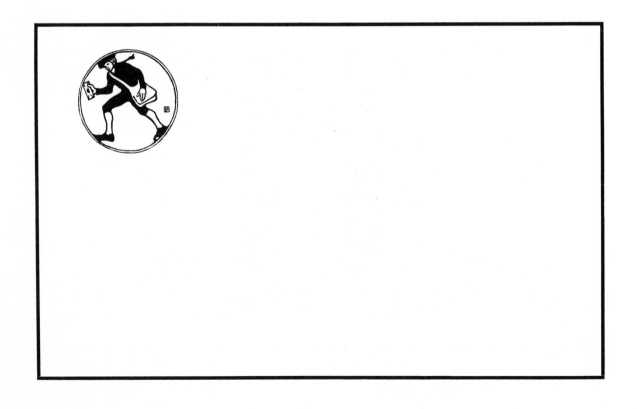

FRANZ STEINER  **HOFLIEFERANT**
TAPEZIERER UND DEKORATEUR · DRESDEN · BLASEWITZERSTR. 9

SCHRIFTSTELLER=VERBAND · ORTSGRUPPE BADEN=BADEN

AUGUST ERICH  BRANDMÜLLER

EINRAHMUNG VON BILDERN · HAUPTZWEIG: GOLDLEISTEN

HERZOGLICHE HOFGLASEREI · MEININGEN, GEORGENSTR. 28

Brauereivereinigung  Nürnberg und Fürth

Mitglied des Schutz-Verbandes · für die Brauereien Deutschlands

---

Allgemeine Eisenbahn=Schlafwagen=Gesellschaft

Hauptkontor Berlin=Charlottenburg

Fernsprecher Amt X 41 · Geschäftsstelle Charlottenburgerstraße 110

KUNSTGEWERBLICHE SCHLOSSEREI VON

GEORG HERNINGER

MÜNCHEN-GLADBACH-EISENBAHNSTR. 167

FERNSPR.: 31 · TELEGR.-ADRESSE: HERNINGER-M.-GLADBACH

Gustav Barnecke
Seilerwaren-Handlung
Charlottenburg
Wilhelminenplatz 11

Rechnung für _____

DROGERIE	**EMPFANGSSCHEIN**	
	MARK_____	
	VON_____	
	ERHALTEN ZU HABEN, BESCHEINIGT	
W. HERBER		

Schuh-Haus HEINRICH MENZINGER, Mannheim

QUITTUNG

Für Herrn _____

TAG	AN WAREN	Mk.	Pf.

DANKEND ERHALTEN SCHUH–HAUS HEINRICH MENZINGER, MANNHEIM

ARCHITEKTUR-
BUCHHANDLUNG
C. BURCKE
BRAUNSCHWEIG
LUDWIGSPLATZ

LIEFERUNGSZETTEL Nr. _____

FÜR HERRN _____

AUF IHRE BESTELLUNG SENDEN WIR IHNEN HIERMIT DIE
UNTENSTEHEND ANGEFÜHRTEN LEHRBÜCHER UND WERKE

TANZORDNUNG

Walzer
Polka
Rheinländer
Walzer (Damenwahl)
Polka
Rheinländer
Schlittſchuhläufer
Schottiſch
Kreuzpolka
Schlußtanz

FRANKFURTER ALPENVEREIN 2. WINTERFEST IM LORKSCHEN KONZERTHAUS

TANZKARTE

WALZER
POLKA
RHEINLÄNDER
WALZER
SCHOTTISCH
POLKA
RHEINLÄNDER
GALOPP

Speisen=Folge

Kraftbrühe

Schleie in Butter

Kalbsrücken gespickt

Junger Gänsebraten

Eingemachte Früchte

Fürst Pückler

Butter und Käse

SPEISEN

HÜHNER-SUPPE

HECHT IN BUTTER

GESCHMORTE RINDSLENDE

WILDSCHWEINS-KOPF

MASTHUHN

DUNSTOBST, SALAT

ERDBEEREIS

NACHTISCH

KÄSESTANGEN

PREISVERZEICHNIS FEINER KRISTALLGLÄSER

KRISTALLGLAS-INDUSTRIE IM ERZGEBIRGE

MOZART- FREUNDE

MITGLIEDS- KARTE N.60

AUF ALLERHÖCHSTEN BEFEHL IM KÖNIGLICHEN OPERNHAUSE AM DONNERSTAG DEN 5. MAI 1908

FIDELIO

PERSONEN

Don Fernando . . . Herr Schmitt	Rocco . . . . Herr Kalmer
Don Pizarro . . . . Herr Ginckel	Marcelline . . . . . Frl. Berchner
Floreftan . . . . . . Herr Danner	Jaquino . . . . Herr Gönner
Leonore (Fidelio) . Frl. Schrader	Soldaten, Volk, Staatsgefangene

ANFANG 8 UHR   ENDE 11 UHR

DER INTENDANT: VON DER HEYD

NEUE FREIE BÜHNE

ERSTER SOPHOKLES-ABEND AM FREITAG DEN 20. SEPTEMBER 1908

OEDIPUS

ÜBERSETZUNG VON GEORG THUDICHUM

PERSONEN

Oedipus . . . . Herr Weidner   Kreon . . . . Herr Gebhard
Jokaſte . . . . Frau Franklin   Teirefias . . . . . . Herr Henckell
Prieſter, Bote, Hirte, Diener, zwei Kinder, Chor

BEGINN 7 UHR   **ENDE 10 UHR**

Franz Grillparzer
Gedenkfeier
zum 50 jährigen Todestage

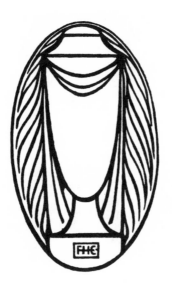

Vereinigung der Österreichischen Schriftsteller
Wien

SCHUTZVERBAND
DER SCHRIFTSTELLER
IN DEUTSCHLAND
ÖSTERREICH
UND IN DER
SCHWEIZ

BERICHT
HERAUSGE=
GEBEN DURCH
DEN ZWEIG=VEREIN
BERLIN·BEARBEITET VON
DR.KARL HEIM UND MAX ELLER

Ew. Hochwohlgeboren

teilen wir hierdurch mit, daß wir mit dem 1. Oktober dieses Jahres den Betrieb der rühmlich bekannten Pfälzer Bier- und Weinstuben übernommen haben. Auch verschänken wir, wie unsere Vorgänger, außer dem einheimischen Bier noch Münchener Löwenbräu und Pilsener Urquell vom Faß, sowie Weine der bekanntesten Pfälzer Firmen in den besten Jahrgängen und in auserlesener Reinheit.

Eine gute, den höchsten Anforderungen genügende Küche wird zu allen Tageszeiten eine abwechselungsreiche Speisenaus- wahl bereit halten; sie sei besonders für Festessen und Familien- feierlichkeiten empfohlen, für welche Zwecke wir auch eine An- zahl größerer und kleinerer Räume neu eingerichtet haben.

Gebrüder Hamm ∙ Kaiserslautern

Die diesjährige Hubertusjagd unseres
Vereins wird am Freitag den 1.November
auf dem Gelände zwischen Laufamholz
und Unterbirg in den Freiherrlich von
Hallerschen Waldungen stattfinden. Die
Mitglieder treffen am Vorabend in Lauf=
amholz, Gasthaus zum Goldenen Engel
ein. Gäste können nur nach vorheriger
Anmeldung eingeführt werden.

Jagdverein Noris

Einladung zum SCHIFFERBALL

Stettin, 23. März 1908 im Konkordia-Saale

PROGRAMM
ZUR RHEINFAHRT DES KÖLNER LEHRERBUNDES AM 2. SEPTEMBER 1907 NACH UTRECHT, HOLLAND

Busse · Hoflieferant

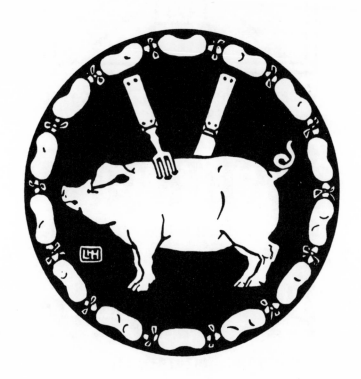

München · Imhofplatz 16
Warenlieferungen frei ins haus

Wir empfehlen uns zur Lieferung von
Heizmaterial bei ermäßigten Preiſen

Steinkohle

das vorzüglichſte und ausgiebigſte
Brennmaterial, geringe Rückſtände

Preßkohle

von größter Heizkraft, für Dampf-
keſſel und andere Heizungsanlagen

Holzkohle

in verſchiedenen Sorten vorhanden
Eigenes Geleiſe · Große Lagerplätze

Gebr. Finck

Wir empfehlen unſere
vorzüglichgearbeiteten

Viktoria-Tiegeldruckpreſſen

zum Drucken, Prägen und
Stanzen in verſchiedenen
Größen und Ausführungen

Viktoria-Spezial-Modell

in unerreichter techniſcher
Ausführung und Bauart

Buchdruck-Schnellpreſſen

und die Erzeugniſſe unſrer

Gravier-Anſtalt

Jlluſtrierte Kataloge und
Muſter auf Verlangen

Maſchinenfabrik

Rockſtroh & Schneider Nachf. A. G.

Dresden-Heidenau

HENCKELL TROCKEN
HENCKELL TROCKEN
HENCKELL TROCKEN
HENCKELL TROCKEN

HENCKELL TROCKEN
HENCKELL TROCKEN
HENCKELL TROCKEN
HENCKELL TROCKEN

BEGRÄBNISANSTALT FRIEDE

Bei Trauerfällen empfehlen wir uns zur Übernahme aller vorkommenden Arbeiten. Lieferung von Särgen in jeder Ausführung. Beerdigungen sowie Leichenüberführungen nach anderen Orten finden pünktliche und gewissenhafte Erledigung.

TYPOGRAPHISCHE VEREINIGUNG ZU WILHELMSHAVEN

Einen Vortrag über die moderne Reklame wird Herr Dr. Peter Jessen aus Berlin am Montag den 10. Oktober im großen Saale des Hotels »Kaiser Friedrich« halten. Zu diesem Vortrage, der durch Auslage von künstlerischen Druckarbeiten und durch Lichtbilder erläutert wird, find Sie hierdurch eingeladen. Der Zutritt ist nur gegen Vorzeigung beiliegender Karte gestattet.